salmonpoetry

ALSO BY NEIL SHEPARD

Scavenging the Country for a Heartbeat
(First Book Award, Mid-List Press, 1993)

I'm Here Because I Lost My Way (Mid-List, 1998)

This Far from the Source (Mid-List, 2006)

(T)ravel / Un(t)ravel (Mid-List, 2011)

Vermont Exit Ramps (Big Table, 2012)

Hominid Up

NEIL SHEPARD

salmonpoetry

Published in 2015 by
Salmon Poetry
Cliffs of Moher, County Clare, Ireland
Website: www.salmonpoetry.com
Email: info@salmonpoetry.com

Copyright © Neil Shepard, 2015

ISBN 978-1-908836-95-3

All rights reserved. No part of this publication may be reproduced or transmitted in any form or by any means, electronic or mechanical, including photography, recording, or any information storage or retrieval system, without permission in writing from the publisher. The book is sold subject to the condition that it shall not, by way of trade or otherwise, be lent, resold or otherwise circulated without the publisher's prior consent in any form of binding or cover other than that in which it is published and without a similar condition, including this condition, being imposed on the subsequent purchaser.

COVER ARTWORK: A detail of John Gurche's *Tower of Time*, used by permission of John Gurche and by the Museum of Natural History, Washington, DC

COVER DESIGN & TYPESETTING: *Siobhán Hutson*

Printed in Ireland by Sprint Print

For Kate and Anna

Acknowledgments

Poems from this manuscript appear in the following magazines: *Anthology of TV Poems*: "No"; *Barrow Street*: "Duration of the Hopi"; *Brilliant Corners: A Jazz Journal*: "Am I Blue," "Joe Louis & the Duke," "L'Heure Bleu," "Wayne & Bud" The Last LP," "Beaufort, SC"; *Chautauqua Literary Review*: "Iced Tea on Deer Isle"; *Cimarron Review*: "Riches"; *Colorado Review*: "The Preparation"; *The Common*: "Excoriating Ghosts"; *Contemporary Poems of New England Anthology*: "From Hayden's Shack I Can See to the End of Vermont"; *I-70 Review*: "One More Thing," "Andy Goldsworthy"; *Long Island Anthology*: "Fear in Northwest Harbor," "Southwest Harbor"; *Louisville Review*: "Stone Giant"; *Mead*: "The Ailment"; *Manhattan Review*: "Street: Video Installation"; *New Ohio Review* (NOR): "Hominid Up"; *North American Review*: "At the Corner of Broadway & 105th"; *Occupy Wall Street Anthology*: "Occupy Wall Street"; *Per Contra*: "Uncle Arthur: The Nuclear Option"; *Poem-a-Day* (Academy of American Poets): "Blustery"; *Provincetown Arts Magazine*: "Meadow Cove Cottage"

I would like to thank Jay White, Tony Whedon, Kate Riley, and Anya Hunter for their close reading of the manuscript and their invaluable suggestions for its improvement. I would also like to thank Poets House and The Writers Room, two urban literary centers where several of these poems were first composed, and the MacDowell Colony and the Virginia Center for the Creative Arts, where the final drafts were accomplished. Thanks also to my colleagues in the Wilkes University MFA Writing Program, but especially to Christine Gelineau, Tony Morris, and Kevin Oderman for their support of my work over many years. Finally, deep gratitude to my partner in life, Kate Riley, for her love and support in the realms of the imagined and the real.

Contents

I. The Ailment

II. Blackfly Poetics

I.

The Ailment

HOMINID UP

I write at night when the old hominid
climbs up to the highest branch of the brain

and crouches there in a leafy crotch
listening to the night-sounds snarling below…

his heart outracing the big cats of the savannah.
He's glad I'm civilized and live indoors,

far from the tooth and claw. Glad my central
plumbing works, my TP dispenser full,

so he doesn't have to shit off a limb.
And though he loves roosting with birds,

the wind rocking him, talking through the mouths
of leaves, he loves also how the birds have

been stuffed into the softest down pillows
where he may lay his head and dream. Dreams

are scarce as water-holes where he's from,
one eye always open for danger, one

for hunger. We're kin for sure: the old beast
in me sleeps lightly or barely sleeps.

I wake often and watch him scratch himself
with a twig that could pass for a pencil

or poke at a moon-lit line of ants that
resembles this scratched pentameter.

Some nights we almost meet at a forking branch
where he chooses silence, and I, this speech.

AT THE CORNER OF BROADWAY AND 105TH

a voice said *Can you help me?* And being new
to the city I turned – to the man twisted
against his walker, spittle on his lip,
sweaty snarls of hair against his forehead –
Can you help me? And he pointed to the unstable
wheels of his walker, the whole con-
trap-
tion of it – I stopped
to help him cross the street, but –
no, I'm sick with HIV, I need a cab
to Beth Israel. And he showed me an I.D. card
to prove his claim. And he showed me six dollars
in his hand. And Beth Israel was way downtown,
another ten or twenty dollars away, and would I
help him? – I could almost hear the hiss
of a kneeling bus, like a great elephant
or camel lowering itself to let the lesser
one ride... but I knew nothing of routes
and caravans and shepherding
him forward... I could hear the subway's whoosh
and rattle beneath us ...but those long stairs downward...
and I could see the lively yellow cabs glowing vacant
up and down the avenue – *I'm not kidding, buddy.*
I really need help – And the more my mind considered
how he'd arrived here with a broken wheel, where he'd been
going in the first place, the more I said *no, no, I can help you*
across the street, and no further. And I saved twenty bucks,
and I wasn't suckered, but later, I felt a swindler's pride,
as if I'd cheated him of his valuables, and later still,
my mind hit a black mood, and I felt a long gray trunk
reach down, and lift me up, and look at me with ancient eyes,
and squeeze the life out of me, and put me down again,
and give me a little nudge homeward with its withered trunk.

THE AILMENT

'Scuse me for coughin on the sidewalk
says the gray-faced woman comin at me
w/a cig on her lip, and it sticks there,

like a sidekick who can't quit her, as she sputters
and – no hands – slips another drag. *'Scuse me*
for spreadin the ailment. And she's music –

the whole phrase, but that quaint
noun, *ailment*, a mild illness,
a kind of pain given as it is gotten,

intransitive become transitive, as in
Because you ail, you ail me.
A thing from which we might all recover:

as we recover the kindred sound
of pain – *āgh* – *ache* a cousin of *day*,
heard the live-long day as a cough that won't

kill us, that casual adjective, *live-long*,
now fully operative, and what ails us –
catarrh, or chilblain from Christmas

panhandling or throat-sore from shouting
Love! and Hallelujah! over a subway grate
to passersby who might toss a coin, float

a dollar – won't kill us, if the money comes,
won't let us ail, while the smell of chocolate
bread drifts from a bakery and jazz pours

from a Sunday brunch, and small ripples
of laughter wash out a café door.

STREET, Manhattan

(Video installation, Metropolitan Museum)

My intention was to give the dreamlike impression of floating through a city full of people frozen in time, caught Pompeii-like, at a particular moment of thought, expression, or activity…a film to be viewed 100 years from now.

—JAMES NARES

True: Slow-mo makes of motion… poetry …
I'm not talking slow-mo dunks or alley-oops,
nor wide receivers rising toward a floating pigskin.

I'm talking summer in suspension, Manhattan, 2011,
high definition camera built for speed – hummingbird wing-
beat, bullet torque – shooting from a roving car pedestrians

as they stand or amble, stride or jog on city sidewalks.
Developed. Slowed to motionlessness. Almost. Frieze
of clerks upholding their scrolls of

papyrus in Egypt's ancient courts. Gesture of grasping
arms or straining legs celebrating some foot-race or wrestle
3000 years forgotten but inked on Greek

amphoras so shoulders might balance the victorious
spoils, virgin olive oil, home to savor 40 days and 40 nights.
Right down to now, or nearly now, Robert

Frank's roving men outside a city bus station,
smoking and blinking, a language of thinking without thinking.
Or Walker Evans' downward-gesturing

farmers whose hands delineate the swirling dust
beneath their feet. All this as precursor to Nares'
loop of motion, scene after scene slowed

to the speed of poetry, discovery of the animating
impulse in human movement, the vaporous thing
that breathes us into being, stride after stride, gesture

on gesture, that doles disgrace or dignity to our least mis-
step or grimace, eye-blink or hair-toss, change of gait or height.
A hand raised toward the street, for want of a caption, could be

surrendering, hailing a cab, waving goodbye. V for victory
or the farthest stretch of fingers desiring a smoke?
Hair sprung from the head sideways, as if the neck were turning

at a backfire, missed street sign, or someone calling her name.
The myriad gazing upward, whether godhead or high-rise or
        whirling
rotor of a copter. What we don't notice in the normal push-

and-pull of human action, or what we read, unconsciously,
in the silent language of the body, we see in a Nares moment,
exposed, extended – slow transformation of a grin

to a grimace, impossible to miss; the swift turn of a man's
head, as beauty flounces by, is now arrested to glacial inspection,
painful to witness, how the jerk is, almost literally, "jerked around"

as if *beauty* were magnetic, as if the nose were hooked
by a scent, and *flounce* shimmers each of its improbable threads
of a summer skirt or wind-blown blouse to the transparent

eyeball that opens on this slowed-down world…how, finally,
it is youth (the younger the quicker) that observes
the observer, discovers the high-speed camera

driving by and follows it with an accusing finger
in a long, slow unspooling of moods, curious, querulous,
musing, accusing, turning the lens back upon the artist

no longer invisible behind a blind but blinded
by the youngest of the company, who must see
every detail still as in a timeless present,

frameless, that exists and exists until the observing eye,
car and camera, turn a corner and drift
out of view, out of mind…

WOMAN CROSSING BROADWAY AT 106TH

There's a woman crossing Broadway against
the light. Dark-skinned, she's wearing a white
summer dress, one of two New York colors
on a summer's day, the other color, black,
equally sexy and chic, but night-savvy,
and now, it's mid-day, so she's wearing white,
smoking a cigarette, clicking along on high
heels, casual as the solstice day is long. The day
is dark, lines of thunderstorms covering
the sun, one darker than the next, making up
their own rules of light, sparking the air
from within a black turbulence. On the avenue,
a mess of mangled umbrellas, blouses
doused to diaphanous surprise, breasts or
bras revealed. Her high heels hobble her
a little. Umbrella-less she lets the rain
arrange her hair, mascara, dimple
her padded shoulders. She crosses amidst
a burst of thunderbolts, ground-strokes making
the street-lights crackle. Gutters gurgle
in the downbursts. A few wan, wet pedestrians
dash past her, splashing her thighs. She seems
to rise higher in the crossing, holding her cigarette
straight out, as if there were a line between
raindrops, a beam she could follow, a thin wire
of sure pleasure she could walk across to the other side.

ERSATZ CATS

Once they were feral creatures
stalking the pastures, or stock-still, with an eye
for the kill. Lately, their gazes glaze, blurred by
a lateral and a sibilant. Can't wrap their tongues
around a hiss. Rheumy eyes of elders. Clipped claws.
Stares vacant as the city apartment they inhabit.
At least, when they were country-cats,
they'd stare at a corner as if it *meant* something:
Coroner. Two sides of a casket. Those cats
had a semiotic sense of wonder, foreboding. Before
this meaningless sentence in the city. Now they've lost
the knack for that hacksaw from the prison
of the literal. Lost that analogic magic: calico
con with a badass black mark over her eye;
her sister, a sleek mottled movie star.
Now they're tub-o-lards, fat cats
in a city of fat cats. And that's no figure
of speech. That's a fat, literal fact, fattened
as a velar calf. No cause for prodigals
to return. Home is where the bones
are after you've stripped the feathers
or fur. No ersatz cat can do that. No
self-respecting meowl, but a low
groan like the grumbles of old men.
Rain hits the windows, and the cats
listen. Lots of knocks. Rain. Radiator. Tango
dancer tossing off his shoes upstairs
and bearing down on the floorboards.
God, we're bored. The cats underfoot
like inert, furry mats, their doleful faces
plopped on their paws. Ersatz cats.

RICHES

I have watched the sunken TV rise
from the panelled foot-board and assume its place
in the room, a black orb that throws off light.
I have raised and lowered it, refusing
the empire's blue glare. I have bathed
in the tub of Lebanon cedar, anointed myself
with oils and emollients, and descended
to the sunken living room. I have dipped
the chilled shrimp in the sundae dish bloodied
with cocktail sauce, and poured into the fluted
blue wine-glass the ancient Bordeaux. I have counted
these as payment, and have, with my writing fingers,
dimmed down the house-lights. I have opened
the windows onto the Atlantic, seen the sweep of the shore,
the sand backed by beach mere, beach mere by bulkhead
and storm-fence, and these by the enormous compound.
And I have listened to the surf's insistent *yes* – the sound
heard long ago near the Dover cliffs, and longer still,
        by the Aegean,
where the laureate in his sponsor's lodge heard the shore's
        slow erosion,
and turned back to the party in his honor, *yes, yes, take it–*
and I have gone out along the cedar boardwalk, from the
        guest-house
to the master's, where the wine was still better, and the
        shrimp more succulent,
and the many courses still awaiting me, amidst the banter
        and the payment
and the praise. And there was so much light, wasn't there,
        thrown off by the rich
discourse on the famous philanthropists, the fabulously ruthless,
and to my question – How long does it take, on a good day,
        to drive
from Manhattan to Easthampton – the smart money said,
        Ten minutes

by helicopter. And to the show-stopping question – If you could try on
one mind throughout human history, whose would it be? – the range
of answers, from Matthew Arnold and Aristotle and Einstein,
to Michaels Jackson and Jordan and Ellen DeGeneres, revealed
the real richness of humans being human. And as the butler dimmed
the chandeliers so the table candles glowed preModernly,
was my face suffused with viands and wines, or was it, when
the post-prandial lights clicked on, quite wan and waxen and wistful
for the long walk back along the cedar shakes, where the grounds crew
would be sweeping up the sand that blows in all night from the ocean, blows
over the bulkhead and beach grass and boardwalk, as if it would bury the world.

OCCUPY WALL STREET

(Saturday, October 15, 2011)

No matter how deftly we death-swoon on the sidewalks
before Bank of America, cops sweep in, sweep us up
for arrest if we lie too long. No matter
how coolly customers withdraw their paltry sums
from Citi Bank or Chase, the chanters
on the sidewalks, in the lobbies, shouting ***Shame!***,
we're cuffed, arrested, tossed into paddy wagons
by the corporation goons. No matter
how the barricades herd us, flocks unwilling
to be fleeced, we compound our voices –
Banks got bailed out; we got sold out!
No matter how they pen us in, keep us out,
crush us in a thick panic, push us to push back –
against cops in riot gear, cops on horseback, cops
with batons and pepper-spray – no
matter. It is spirit, not matter, lifting us
from our common squalor – ***The people, united,***
will never be defeated! – spirit that spreads us
around the planet – in Sydney and Tokyo,
London and Rome, Rio and Toronto – spirit
gone viral – ***We are the 99% !*** –
and there is no realm beyond the satellites
where all's accounted for, there is nothing
but our world, under the downsizing sun
and imploding stars, spinning in the black
expanse of the universe, the endless
sums and shares, and the immaterial
voices of witness that say, *There is*
another world, and it is in this one.

JOE LOUIS AND THE DUKE

It was June 22, 1938, at the Savoy.
It was active duty and Hitler blackening
the Alps with the long shadows of *Ubermenschen*.
From Fort Lee, New Jersey, to the Harlem clubs was a bridge
or a tunnel away – a span across that black Hudson starred
with city lights, or a dark dig beneath the river lit with carbon
arcs – some transport across that dark, dividing water. A free pass
from the base, a barracks bus, and I was there, jazzed

up, one of the few white guys in the club, and felt it, but felt black
as any welt, felt bruised and leathered as any fighter.
Earlier, I'd sat in the cheap seats of Yankee Stadium, watching
The Fight, the impossible, the slow German, Max Schmeling,
        knocked down
by lightning-fast Joe Louis in the first and only round,
        knocked down
and out. Now I knew what was possible. Now my ears popped

with Duke Ellington on the bandstand, all that false nobility
for real, whether it was Count or Duke
or Lady Day – and I had seen them in satin
earlier that night, at The Fight, Duke and Cab Calloway,
and Tallulah Bankhead, all feathered and bannered
and royal blues and purples, and as Schmeling fell
to his knees, unable to rise again, the Bismarck sunk,
the UBoats swamped, Helmiss cried *Unmoglich!* (Impossible!)
and Tallulah jumped up and screamed to the Schmeling fans,
"I told you, you sons of bitches!"and waved her peacock
plumes in their faces, those magnificent fragile eyes! –

so that, back at the Savoy, I was hardly surprised
to see The Brown Bomber jaunt in
who had just fought Hitler and Hess and Goebbels and
the Super-Race, and had destroyed it

from the opening bell – the fight lasted only 2 minutes,
Schmeling threw only 2 punches, he went down twice, and all
the hateful binary combinations of good/evil, white/black,
master/slave,
came crashing down with the 1-2 combinations off Joe's fists –
and the great white hope lay sprawled on the canvas
like a bloody swastika – and everybody turned

as the King, Joe Louis, with his entourage
dressed to the tuxedoed nines, but with his royal purple
boxing robe and hood
still draped over his head, walked, skipped, double-stepped,
all footwork and combinations, left jab, right cross, uppercut,
and up

came Duke's horns, up the drum roll, up the piano's segregated
white and black notes, the Duke pounding them together in wrist-
snapping arpeggios, smashing those separations with blue notes,
crossing over from black to white and white to black – and down
went that great white hope, that thing shadowing the Alps,
down and out.

WAYNE & BUD

Hip new kid on the bandstand, Wayne Shorter, way back
in '59, already thoughtful and silent, and when he spoke,
he spoke no evil, just words of cosmic good, insane
one-liners, so spaced they needed warp speed
to connect, or if he didn't speak, he played those smart interstellar
phrasings from soprano sax, brassier concatenations from tenor –
and that first night, Wayne, on the bandstand with lithe Miles,
Paul Chambers, Jimmy Cobb, and a glazed Bud
Powell at the keyboards, Bud just gazed, gazed off,
        as Wayne chorused.
After the gig, well along in his addictions, Powell stumbled
to Wayne's digs. A slight arpeggio
against the door, Wayne opened, and in walked Bud. Straight
past him, crashed in a chair, and just stared, stared hard.
Then, to Wayne's "What's up?" said, "Play me that thing you
        played tonight
on *Budo*." And Wayne played it again, but never the same,
so made it jump again. And Bud just said,
Unnh huh. And walked out. And seven lean years later,
toward the end of his swooning pianissimo,
Bud finally told him – I was just checking
to see if Jazz would be okay, after I'm gone, and it will be, Budo.
And then he checked out.

L'HEURE BLEU

You can almost hear the spiralling phrases
of Lester Young's last gig in Paris as they empty
from his horn in the blue hour, the whole history
of jazz blowing from the Blue Note over
café tables where you sit with the ghosts
of Sartre and Camus arguing the suicidal blues…

and the blueness of the blue hour brightens whatever mood
steered Sidney Bechet here after the Great War to light up
the City of Light with a Dixie beat; steered Bud Powell here,
beyond the graves of Normandy, to empty
his addictions into the piano's white rush.

You can hear Lady Day's voice shot full of booze, full
of bruises at the Mars Club on Rue de Rivoli, or Billy Strayhorn
and the Duke polishing a few brighter tunes, scored
for the film *Paris Blues*. You can hear Quincy Jones, Bobby Few,
and another dozen jazz emigres, who found the happy hour

of America bluer than blue… and whatever steered
Baker or Bricktop or Johnny Griffin to these streets
steers you now to a jazz club in a cul de sac,
where the blue hour dilutes your mood with a few drinks
to the good, until there's a halo around your head –

Tonight you sit at a café table and watch the French
linked arm-in-arm – for all their brazen
debate and haughty talk, you love them
for the warm home they gave jazz in its bluest hours –
you raise a glass of Bordeaux and watch them light up

and stumble off across cobblestone, toward a moon
stained yellow as a smoker's fingernail, as if a cigarette
answers the blue hour's question of jazz-decline
with glowing tracers in the dark, and leads beyond
the blue hour, toward the next glass of wine,
lifted, toasted, drained.

THIS IS A TEST, CAN YOU HEAR ME?

This is a test, can you hear me?
This is a test, a call of distress, can you hear me?

This is the blues, the rhythm I choose, can you hear me?
This is the blues – my baby, my baby, and my baby –
They all done me wrong. They all gone away – can you hear me?

I know you got your heartache. I can hear you.
I know you got troubles way down in your shoes. I do, too.
I can hear you, I can hear you. Can you hear me?

This is a test. You gonna take it too.
Gonna feel bluer than blue, lower than low-down.
Can you hear me? I'm at that age

when the woman I loved with raven hair
has a head of gray. When the one with the perfect pear
breasts has rotten nectar, a bee sting, a cancer.

When her pearl of a smile shines at night
from a water glass. When that piece of ass
is now just a piece of a more comprehensive ass.

Can you hear me? I'm at that age when Love
says, Put up or shut up. Get it up, or put it
down! I'm talking that deepest-down thing:

Love, when the body's gone. Love with the blonde
washed out, the blue rinsed in. That's the blues
Lovers choose. Can you hear me? Can you

hear me? This is a test. You're gonna take it, too.

THE LAST LP

in my jazz collection was *Kind of Blue*,
snagged from a Woolworth's bin –
dental floss, hair brush, Harlequin
romance, floppy slippers, and old LPs –
all for under a buck! and I plucked up
from under a 3-pak of panties, Fruit
of the Loom, that blue-black album:

There was Miles moody against a black
background blowing his silver horn,
eyes lidded, nose flared, lips pursed
to educate the air with a pensive phrase –
no dazzle with a bright blast or field-holler.
No... Cool, muted, understated, and under-
stood: that silence hung at the edge

of all he did, shaped every note
blown into space and time,
ready to take back
any place the breath refused
to fill. And in tribute
to that silence, Miles added
his own: All that muted brooding

lacquered the black album cover,
shaded the names of the giants –
Adderly, Evans, Coltrane, Kelly –
not popped from the black
by a fine white font, but varnished,
yellowed, some half-diminished thing,
and one blue phrase enlarged, *Kind of Blue* –

and further down that remainder bin, beneath
the yoyos and tissues and miniature Army men,
I found *Crying in the Cheap Seats*, the first
book of my jazz-poetry teacher, Bill
Tremblay. Impossible!—that same man
who had turned me on to Miles
and showed me the value of silence

when the game was rigged, and the rich
had so much, and the rest had less, unless –
if they listened, if they searched, they might find
fortune in the lowliest places, in the cheap
seats and remainder bins. Impossible!
That someone looking to floss his teeth
or brush her hair would find poetry

and jazz so dark, so common anybody
could put down that brush and cry
or else floss till the plaque burned
and the blood came and never stop
trying to clean out that silence
from the mouth that says *I'm Crying*
in the Cheap Seats and I'm Kind of Blue.

AM I BLUE

(April 5, 2005)

I'm blue politics, blue state
of mind, can't sashay my way
through the minefields of red states' war-
chatter, where Bush owns the lane, the paint, the Great

Plains and the deep red reserves of South.
I'm blue because Bob Creeley died last night
in the great blue state of Massachusetts,
and he was the birth of Verse's cool, conducting

a blue cigarette and a steering wheel
in a compact car, driving the brain light-
speed through minimalist
lines that always broke
down, that said, I
knew a man, and he
was blue.

And blue has no place to go except out –
out of this poem, out of this world, to rise into sky
and look down on a rush of red confusion,
and get it, get it good, let a blue whistle part the lips,

and say, man – man, man, man – am I blue.

ELECTION DAY: Nelson County, Virginia

(November 4, 2008)

Door-hanging, is what they called it at headquarters.
Take a flyer, take a partner, take precaution.

We drove down a crumbling hilltop road called Main Street,
kudzu creeping over the tar. Broken

shacks, trailers with buckled roofs, yards buried
in trash. Off the spine of Main, roads collapsed

in weedy paths spilling east to the six-lane,
west to the flood plain. Houses with no

doorknobs, no doors, nothing
from which to hang the blue sign promising *Change*.

Yet each had a glowing *Keep Out* sign and a couple
of snarling dogs. If I saw it this way,

it was the way I was raised
to see it. Forgive me if we didn't visit every home, hang

the sign on every knob, saying we'd been there and wanted
their vote because it meant a lot to their future.

Watching a few kids listless on the stairs, I could see
how far we'd let them fall. *Got some spare change?*

they spat, without looking up. They were locked in,
and the best intentions of a black man in a white house

would not spring them. The beautiful
words of the orator would not translate

into language explaining our blue hanging sign on the door –
Vote for Change! – nor their orange reply – *Keep Out!*

OBAMA'S BUMPS IN THE ROAD

(adapted from New York *magazine, culled quotes from Barack Obama's public speeches on the American economy from March 2009 – June 2011)*

There are going to be some bumps in the road
and there are going to be times when people get impatient.
Get impatient. We are going to do every single thing we can
to pull this economy out of the ditch. You would have expected
Republicans would have been willing to help out… and yet
after driving our economy into the ditch, they decided to stand
on the side of the road and watch as we tried to yank it out.
After *they* drove the car into the ditch! We're out there in the mud
pulling the car out of the ditch, and they're sitting there comfortable,
drinking a Slurpee! Now if your teenager drives the car into a ditch,
bangs it up – what do you do? You take the keys away. Those folks
drove the economy into a ditch, and they want the keys back!
And my answer is, No, you can't have the keys. We had to put on
our galoshes, went down there in the mud. And we've been shoving
that car out of the ditch inch by inch. After all our huffing and puffing,
we finally get the car back on the blacktop, on level ground. We've got
mud on our shoes, our back is sore. I don't know whether they were
on their Blackberry while they were driving, or doing something else
irresponsible. Now they want the keys back. Do we give them the keys?
They'll drive right back into the ditch! We have gotten down into
the ditch,
and it was a pretty deep ditch. It was a really deep ditch!
I know Al Franken talked to you a little bit about the analogy
of a car being driven into the ditch – although I guess Al embellished
it a little. He said there were alligators down there. I didn't see
the alligators. But it's true the car went into the ditch, and we pulled
it out. There are always going to be bumps on the road to recovery.
We're going to pass through some rough terrain even a Wrangler
would have a hard time with. This is no exaggeration. There will be
bumps on the road to recovery. But we won't go into a ditch again.

EDISTO ISLAND

(Grove Plantation House, SC)

I'm raising dust on a dirt road to Hollings Wildlife Refuge
where Feds now manage the land. Hand-dug ditches
once drained swamp-water here for human plans, plantations
of rice and cotton and cane, dug and diverted, sun-
up to sundown, malaria to consumption to yellow
fever, the water from the land: impoundments, held
in place by rice trunks, old African ways of trapping
and taming the water. I've passed beyond the man-
grove roots and smooth beggar ticks that clutch the land
and hold it down. Now I'm out of the car, where yellow-rumps
warble in the willows, purple gallinule whistle from still pools. Black
vulture, Sankofa bird, floats over, shadow like an arrow
pointing far off toward the hills. Run from the dogs,
the masters. Collapse or die, vulture carry you home.
Se wo were fi na wosankofa a yenkyi. I'm standing
ten feet from a scum-green alligator, bulbous nose, eyes open
and eyeing me. Flat water, flat land, under an oppressive sky,
the world so prone I'd feel crushed, if not for the sun-sparkle,
the far-off hills, the water lit to the land's circumference. Field-
glasses in hand, I eye birds passing through shadows, field-
hands floating among the birds, still circling in thermals.

* *Sankofa* is an Akan (West African) term that literally means, "to go back and get it." One of the Adinkra symbols for Sankofa depicts a mythical bird flying forward with its head turned backward. The egg in its mouth represents the "gems" or knowledge of the past upon which wisdom is based; it also signifies the generation to come that would benefit from that wisdom. This symbol often is associated with the proverb, "*Se wo were fi na wosankofa a yenkyi,*" which translates to, "It is not wrong to go back for that which you have forgotten."

MID-MARCH, BEAUFORT, SOUTH CAROLINA

I wanted warmth and blue estuaries and not a living care.
Wanted t-shirts and shorts before the sand-fleas spawned.

I wanted salt on the tongue and salt in the darkness
of the throat, where smell conspires with taste,

where we judge what we like out of the acids
and sweetness of the world and give it names.

I wanted the old brackishness that says
there's an ocean over the dune

and a ship sailing from a long way off, carrying
cargo in the hold that will build whatever empire

in the sand I can imagine. I could smell the old
confederacy of magnolia and wisteria blooming

on the porches of mansions, one rumored to be
the site of *The Great Santini*, another of *Glory*,

whatever era, whatever film required live
oaks and Spanish moss by the boat-load

and plantation homes surrounded by blue estuaries.
The oldest church had the oldest pews and DARS

proud of their ancestors – even those
who'd banned Marian Anderson from singing

on some Easter Sunday long ago in Constitution Hall.
I smelled the land risen up

from swamps, risen on the backs of black
labor that drained, channeled, tilled, planted –

rice as they had known back home, or later, cotton,
spun into the white shirts for Sunday prayer.

From the church, where whites once sat downstairs,
nearer the preacher, and blacks sat upstairs,

nearer to God, I could see the spot where the slave-
ships once slipped into this harbor.

Out another window, I saw the mounds under which
the unnamed dead made the earth rise up.

TRACKING BIRDS AND GULLAH SPEAKERS

(mid-March, South Carolina)

This morning, coastal fog clots the binoculars. Brown pelican?
Storm Petrel? Field-glasses tear with moisture. Masked Booby?
Maybe

it's better in the salt marsh – Godwit, Clapper Rail – but the tide's out,
the marsh just mudflats, the birds further out where fish flash and dive.

Bird tracks lead a few feet, vanish into thin air, where the winged ones rose up.
I wait them out. Soon enough, time turns the tide and brings them in…

salt lagoon alive now with great blue and little blue and sun enough to dry
my lenses, brighten their wind-lifted feathers. It's all about patience, friends! –

knowing how to hunker down or hide in a bird blind. Later, I lunch
at a Shrimp Shack and spy on a few old salts, two blacks who look to speak

the local creole: Gullah. While I lift my field-glasses toward the bay
where ospreys cry and dive, I eavesdrop on the old ones: they speak

shrimp-boat, tide-channel, and rising costs of shrimp-baskets, deep-fried. Perfect
English. I take a second lunch at Gullah Grub cafe, a seafood-bisque thick with

sand, but not a Gullah word spoken. *Nyam*. Two teenaged blacks
say their mamas
speak it, their grandmamas speak it good, but they, only in snatches.
Talk to granny,

outside, they say, weaving straw hats and baskets…but granny won't
give a God-blessed word of Gullah,
not a cursed, white-betrayed word in Gullah, though she'll sell
me a basket

and point me toward the museum, Penn Cultural Center on
St. Helena's Island,
where the schooling of Gullah slaves began, and later, where
the nonsense, the pidgin

spit out so quick it was gibberish, was captured on reel-to-reel,
recorded, located –
a funeral dirge sung in Sierra Leone. The language you cry in

is the language of home, says the man at the Penn Center,
who says, no,
he don't speak Gullah good enough to speak it to me, *buckruh*,

but granny, back at Gullah Grub, speaks it *swonguh* and I should
check it out,
and buy a basket, while I'm at it. Yes. So, I wander down a trail
to the bay,

spend an idle hour listening to tall grasses speak their language
along the edge
of the estuary. See a flotilla of manta-ray like clouds beneath
the ocean,

a green heron, a snowy egret, all speaking. Then return to the
museum where,
wonder of wonders, a new curator, just come on duty, sassy, says,

so you wanna learn some Gullah, huh – I like to play with people's minds –
you bird yet on Daufuskie Island, for *pojo* and *cootuh*? What's that? I say.

What's that? And she, never you mind, but mind this. De white man
stole that island from us. Ain't nuthin there but a lot of white folks

in gated places playing golf. You wanna learn? *Da fis key* is put yourself
in de other folks' shoeless shoes. You got it? I got it. No, you ain't got it.

What didn't I get? What was the first key? Take off my shoes? Lower the field
glasses, come out from behind the bird blind? Da fis key is this: you gotta stand

where we be standin. We here on St. Helena. That's home.
You got it? I got it. No, you ain't got it. What didn't I get?

Then she put her hands on my shoulders, said, close your eyes, honey,
and I'm g'wan spin you 'round a few times. I spun. Which way

you facing? I don't know, I said. You got it, she said. No, I don't got it. Yes,
you got it. You don't know which way you facing. You check your compass,

you might say South. But we folks – we who rooted right here in St Helena –
say we rooted right here and we facing toward da fis key south.

And dat's what your white man calls Daufuskie. So dere you go.
Now you know some Gullah and you know how white folks speak

what they don't understand – *gibberish* – into something
        nobody
understands and it wanders further and further from
        understanding, until

they ain't no use at all in tryna teach white folks anything atall.
Now if you want to know a good birding place, I can tell you
        that too.

CRAZY QUILT: DOUBLE ACROSTIC

What could a twelve-year-old slave-gir**L**
Achieve when John Logan said to her, **I**
Like you, Hannah, and so in this spring seaso**N**
Know you're now bound to my daughter, as the **V**

Nests in the W. You're a June wedding gift **I**
Offer her. What could Hannah do – not *anger, heel,*
henna her hair – but fee**L**
Relief. She'd leave the heat of the fields, the cotton hau**L**,
To work as a house servant. (She'd rather *rehang an eel hen*!)
She'd learn to sew, to se**E**
How cotton turned to cloth, and cloth to patched fabri**C**

That one day could be pieced into a crazy quilt, *an angular*
indoor rudder, scraps of aqu**A**,
Orange, brown, or white, speaking like Vai glyphs,
like geese in a migrating **V**

That shift, falter, almost fall apart, then point northward,
arrow-straight, aliv**E**,
High in a boundless sky. Yes, what could Hannah do but
sew an *unerring rural doodad*, sew he**R**
Embroidered pieces into a pattern so scattered it meant
nothing but distractio**N**.

The poem is based on a Crazy Quilt created by Hannah Greenlee in the 1850s and completed by her daughter, Emm Greenlee, in 1896. According to historical record, Hannah pieced this quilt together in McDowell County, North Carolina, during the era of the Underground Railroad when slaves were escaping to the North. She stitched into the pieces African symbols which served as messages and directions to would-be travellers on the "Railroad". Some of the symbols are recognized as characters of the Vai Syllabary, an African alphabet.

Two acrostics: Walk north to the/ Linville Cavern

Anagrams for Hannah Greenlee, Underground Railroad

Found phrases from cut-outs of Wikipedia articles on Crazy Quilt, Vai Syllabary, McDowell County

YOUNG WRITER AT WORK

I'd almost forgotten how a young writer works,
If not confidently, at least ambitiously, awake

All night on a red-eye flight, fresh from a writer's
Conference that fed the fame-machine –

To be, one day, that introspective elder on the retrospective
Panel, young writers gathered to his words – or to be

The keynote speaker, cradling the fame-key in a limp,
Aesthetic hand… Except his is thick and black,

And his head of hair is black and closely cropped.
An ex-Marine, he's somehow found his way

To the shores of poetry. When he grips my hand,
Locks my gaze, and says he wants to be a war-poet,

I can't tell if his stories will be straight and strong,
Or complex stutters and intricate silences.

He's young: probably the former… Later, the latter.
Perhaps his poems will be hobbled in style like the limp

Work of most beginners. Or perhaps he'll burst through
Every road-block with the relentless acceleration

Of the great ones. When he says his buddies died
In Tikrit and he wants to go down to death to save them,

I know he'll need a guide like Komunyaaka or Turner
For the language of triage and carnage. Now he dismisses me

And turns to the task, as if the attack must be launched
Before dawn. His reading lamp glows as he goes it alone –

All night beside me, powering words onto his laptop,
His elbow bumping mine burst after burst. I can feel

The jolt of the poem, the rhythm of each racing line,
And how the spacing bar projects a phrase far

From its kin, far out along the white spaces
Of the page. No matter how tangled his first

Drafts, no matter how an elder's eyes might
Judge them worthy or unworthy, he'll still rescue

His buddies from the roadside bomb.
He'll bark a few short orders, gather them

To his words, and lead them from obliteration.
Perhaps one day he'll be a stern old poet at a lectern…

Or perhaps four gold stars will sparkle on his chest.
Who can say? For now, he says, this is what a nation is:

Boots on the ground, sand in the teeth, that lets
Civilians sleep or dream the lines of poems.

Whether I agree or not, I salute the young
Writer there at his screen, all night probing

The desert road for a flash, a flashback,
A way to bring them home.

SURVIVORS

(text taken and shaken from *New York Times*, January 20, 2010, Dwight Garner reviewing Charles Pellegrino's *The Last Train from Hiroshima*)

He lived through two atomic blasts,
Hiroshima, Nagasaki. Good luck
dogged him. And he wasn't alone:
1 of 165 people who survived
Hiroshima "only to wind up in Nagasaki
when that bomb fell three days later."

They survived thanks to blind fortune.
Sheltered from gamma and infrared death rays,
from flattening blasts, in spots that acted
as "natural shock cocoons." They called
the bomb the *pika-don*, the "flash-bang."
They learned: if you see

and survive the *pika*, you have a few seconds
to duck. The *don* is on its way.
Another lesson: wear white.
Women wearing patterned clothes, say, black flowers
on white cloth, had dark flowers permanently
branded on their skin. Yet another lesson:
bombs behave like microwave ovens,
heating metal until it glows. Those

who wore wristwatches were branded
where metal met skin. Many people
reported the smell of burning human flesh
was similar to the scent of squid when it was grilled
over hot coals, with a few pieces of sweet pork thrown in.

Survivors saw "ant-walking alligators," men and
women "now eyeless and faceless — with their heads

transformed into blackened alligator hides
displaying red holes, indicating mouths."
The alligator people did not scream.
Their mouths could not form the sounds.
The noise they made was worse than screaming.

They uttered a continuous murmur — "like locusts
on a midsummer night. One man, staggering
on charred stumps of legs, was carrying a dead baby
upside down." Those who survived the bomb
were people who ignored others crying out
in extremis or who stayed away from flames,
"even when colleagues shrieked from within them."

Those who stayed where they were, or hid
behind a mound, a hill when the fires spread
and closed in, escaped alive, guided
by the oldest instinct, older
than civilization."And we know it,
we who have survived."

UNCLE ARTHUR: THE NUCLEAR OPTION

Seabrook was his baby. His middle name was safety.
        He could clean his kid's diaper
or a nuclear rod at a moment's notice. He believed in
        Yucca Mountain. He believed
in a junkyard called outer space. His kids would grow up
        greener and wiser.

He was a Sunday painter. He loved the glow of sunset.
        Mountains moved him, mostly
ones of solid granite, far from a fault line. He was
        mild-mannered. Well-traveled. Wry-
humored. He could tell a joke that started with apocalypse
        and ended with zeugma:

the NRC met with the EPA and left the meeting in high spirits
and a Cadillac; the NRC met the NRA at a party and they drank
to their mutual security until they were bombed. Never mind.

He could order a boiled lobster and talk nuclear reactors
        in the same sentence.
He could write his name out of the history books if the
        cooling walls cracked.
He grew up on Three Mile Island, boned up on Alamogordo,
        toured Chernobyl.

He was prepared for a meltdown. He was the good
        Samaritan gone atomic.
He could hear the hum of atoms safe in their reactors.
        He could hear the hum
of children in their little bedrooms, busy as bees. He could
        hear the hum

of bees after nobody heard them. He had that kind of optimism.

DURATIONS OF THE HOPI

Who knows? In time,

once they've charred

the atmosphere, humans

might think of themselves

as actions, not durations.

As in Hopi, *flame*,

meteor, lightning, are brief

visitations, verb's impermanence –

how quickly we burn

the earth – whereas the

passing of *cloud, storm*,

lasts just long enough

to live as nouns –

that recur, recur,

and water the world.

CONNECTICUT

Or like stout Cortez when with eagle eyes
He stared at the Pacific – and all his men
Looked at each other with wild surmise –
Silent, upon a peak in Darien.

–John Keats

Connect the cut in the hills south of North Brookfield
to the bubbling summer wren, the burbling red-wing
dipping asymptotic on spring thermals a math whiz
could graph before the pneumatic gasp of the tour bus
doors open at 2000 psi and fifty birders with life
bird-lists stumble out to check-mark the earliest
arrivals on record (relative to their short lives, relative
to the ages of fire and ice preceding this one).
Connect the cut to wood ducks with Spanish
moss from southern swamps still clinging
to their bills as they follow the transmission lines in,
having flown north to South Norwalk, following the coal-fired
smokestacks warming their white rumps, the algal bloom's
meal of green scum and sulfurous warmth, released

weeks too early, per minute, per hour, per day, increasing
2 degrees Kelvin, molecules ear-marked for May Day now
date-released on April Fools. Connect the cut in the hills
to hundred-dollar haircuts of Connecticut lawyers
down on Connecticut Ave. in D.C. lobbying Congress
for weapons contracts in Windsor Locks, liability limits
for Hartford insurance, national think-tanks in Greenwich,
which can calculate the cost of "clean coal" in eastern
Kentucky, field teams of lawyers to battle black-lung claims
along the grimy towns of the Alleghenies, sweeten NIMBY deals
to keep the oil refineries in New Jersey. Connect it all to transmission
lines carrying the energy in, more birds arriving early from the clear-cut

tropics, arriving over the flyways of Connecticut, over the cut
in the hillsides south of Darien, from a peak Keats never
imagined,
where transformers hum in megawatts and amaze the sky.

NO

We have now, as we had then, clean-shaven men
whose hearts are sixteen, Americans who've seen
death on a scale no greater than the loved one
lapsed in a hospital bed or eased out of a freezer in the town
morgue. Why be morbid? We're young men
until our end, no matter how many blown-
up bodies we've seen on the big screen
or laser-guided missiles a luminous green
as they fall on Baghdad or Tripoli on CNN;
file-footage of charred tanks or human bone,
earthquake, tsunami, meltdown in Japan;
wrapped in wreckage, the clothes of fishermen,
the fishing boat in a tree, the fishermen gone,
a red Toyota truck atop a Yamaha piano,
a crumpled father traveled from Tokyo
to shout into the tumbled house, Yoko, Yoko,
for a daughter swept out to sea, his mouth an O
that should make all clean-shaven men say No,

though their hearts are sixteen.
Hear the plea from the seriocomic newsman,
to do something, please, to ease human
suffering: two catastrophes that conjoin –
Libya and Japan, another bone, and another – and no one,
no one, stops caring about the tiger blood of Charlie Sheen!
(Even the Japanese 100 miles from the radiation zone
turn away from the TV to slurp noodles and complain
of the slowdown in production, turn back when
the weatherman says wind's blowing in their direction.)
The newsman's face crumbles, but tightens
after commercial, the resins re-touched on his skin;
the brow shines, the eyes a lustrous brown
that report from a place hardened
to pain. One can almost hear Auden

with his famous lines on suffering under the sun, oh
how Icarus falls from the sky while children go
elsewhere to play or a plowman sows
his field and figures what the harvest owes –

which was already an anachronism in Auden's time,
        farming un-
done by city industry, the dynamo hum un-
leashed, leashed to coal, petroleum, nuclear fission
to warm our homes. And we clean-shaven
men, at ease in our skin, fresh from American
ablutions, can towel our faces clean,
kiss good morning to our loved ones,
walk outside to a world that is still green,
unlock our cars, climb in, and tune
out the catastrophic news on the radio,
the woe of a woman whose house, like an ice floe,
floated off with her five children frozen in the window,
in her memory, in – but tune it out, tune to music, to
a tune we remember from sixteen,
when the world, and all memory, was green –
not green with radiation, nor gangrene, no,
nothing rotting from a leg-wound or a burn – no,
just good, American green.

STONE GIANT

At first I was hardly involved.
A child snapped its photo in an open field.
It was miles off, perhaps bothering someone else.
But it had its eye on this corner of the pasture too.
The child saw only what appeared to be precarious
Stone upon stone, almost comically unbalanced, like a
 stone wall
Upended, turned vertical, and vertibratic boulders
 soft-clicking
As if applauding its snapped photo. And though it moved
 slowly
And though it was still miles off, its stride, when it strode,
 could cloud
A portion of sky. I must have gone off to another dream,
 this one safe
Enough to leave unmanned, but when I returned the child
 was still there
In a corridor of pasture snapping exposure after exposure
 of the stone giant
Until its stride took it squarely into our space and landed
 with bomb-weight.
Its footprint gouged a trench in the mud, its stone vertebrae
 reverberating strange
Gongs and chimes that deafened us. Then I was involved in
 clutching up
The awe-struck child who had dropped the camera and
 grown stone-dumb
In its presence, and I caught up that child and ran down a
 gauntlet
Of stone walls marking the separations, and not a neighbor
 came
To roll boulders in that giant's way and trip it up, so it
 came on now
Crushing the camera though not really having seen it,
 came on now

Tall as a telephone pole but stony in its gait, nothing warm
in its
Grain or texture, nothing funny about its stony frame
Gray as shadow, casting shadow over our land. Then we turned
And ran from that undefended land down stone steps,
The giant behind us, all of us going down a stone vault
masons had pain-
Stakingly made millennia before us, some time of tumuli
and brief
Allegiances and one's clay beginnings closer to one's stone
endings than this child
And I had known. And we felt a cold wind off the stone giant,
and the enormous
Gonging filled our lungs, and we heard its strange mathematics
coldly marking
The boundaries of our lives, what little time was left.
Ten steps would be
Our end we heard it chime, and soon enough close ahead
we saw the hall dead
End and heard the stone's enormous crush behind us,
upon us, and turned and tried
To scurry under its downturned petrifying limbs and
bumped head
On into its slow inexorable motions and saw to our horror,
as we were
Scraped up and smashed into its grayness, joining the other
carbon forms
Crushed against its petroglyphic chest, it hadn't even seen us.
It had been
Drawn by the glint of the camera, the shiny opportunity,
the small chance
Of light in all that gray expanse of time through which it
endured.

II.

Blackfly Poetics

FEAR IN NORTHWEST HARBOR

(Deer Isle, Maine)

I knew the eagle was coming because of the crows.
I was reading Cormac McCarthy. *The Road*. The end
Of the road, really, post-literate, that ends
At the ash-gray, iodine-smelling sea, millions of fish
Washed up and decomposed to fish-scales –
And the crows told me with their wild caws:
Eagle. They don't fear osprey, only
The eagle's omnivorous appetite.
I looked up from my book, straight up.
Thirty feet overhead, the eagle's
Yellow talons and stern yellow eye.
Its domineering gaze was, indeed,
American, a sun bound to extinction.
In the novel, all the birds are dead as well.
None can fly high enough to pierce the nuclear
Clouds born of the light of a hundred suns…
None can reach the one life-sustaining sun.

SOUTHWEST HARBOR

The sandbar to the island
disappears. But I can see the flash
of field glasses from the mansion,
the owner at high water
approving the sea's separation:

how it closes the circle around his home
and keeps him safe from beachcombers,
who stand and gaze across the high-tide bay
and wait for whatever washes up on the mainland,
a drifting rib of wood, an empty shell, a polished
shard of glass, to keep or sell.

A solitary loon spies me and dives,
surfacing far off. Harbor seals laze beyond the breakers,
on rocky shelves. I wander far down the strand –
hoarding my privacy – as close to the vanished
sandbar as the tide allows.

How can I hoard what I don't own? How can I condone it?
I watch seagulls circle the lobster boats, squawking for a claw
or pulpy bait, the boats floating over fished-out waters.

SUNDAY EVENING, VINALHAVEN

(Penobscot Bay, Maine – for Wallace Stevens)

Vinalhaven, complacencies of lobster,
lime green cocktails and Sunday yachters.
They float over the wide water without sound,
mainsails luffing in intermittent wind.
The crosstrees on their boats like arms of gods
transport them through bays and narrows and could,
if spars were true enough, transport them
through the clouds, or through the island's hem
of roses and Queen Anne's lace, to the very
spot of roods and steeples – more easily
said than done, as is reaching the god's eye
center of the sun, which just now begins
its afterglow, staining the sky golden,
going rose, blood red, burnt siennese.
And one might ask on evenings such as these,
could god be a cod salted on sea wrack,
could he be a shiskabobbed shrimp or scallop,
a mighty mussel on a half shell. In brief,
a thing shorn from the deep, a shared misery
hauled up and sacrificed from the sea.
The yachters slip through our reach without sound,
return to their slips where the night impounds
them. Tomorrow is Monday and lobster
boats will own the harbors, their motors
coughing, a catch in the throat that never
clears, a rasp of buoys and traps and clever
cash to be made on the wharves. They'll stick it
to Sunday sailors, to mainland tourists
who make the ferry crossing and joke
about the locals. If god is a Coke,
they'll sell more communion wine than St. Paul's
on Sunday. If god is a mighty mussel,
they'll harrow the deep for those white wafers

and baste with a bloody sauce for fairweather
Christian tongues. Here comes the last ferry of
the day. Here comes the first fogbank of
the nether hour. Here comes the first shrill blast
of the horn, the oldest warning of lost
purpose, misdirection, isolation,
the golden silence shattered, the vacation
suddenly wobbly, momentarily disturbed
before the next cocktail, the next hors d'oeuvre.

LOBSTER POTS

The thin women at the Fishermen's Festival were sweating
Were boiling lobsters melting butter steaming mussels
Basting corn-on-the-cob turning out these Sunday lunches
For deep-pocket tourists in fat-cat America the richest
Calorie-per-capita nation on this god-starved green
And blue planet or else how to explain the obvious
Half-hitch strung around the descendants of descendants of
Fisherpeople hitched right to the dock right to the lobster
Pots boiling under noon sun while the cruise ships docked
And those without a half-hitch strolled over and ordered
Six clambakes and seven lobsterbakes and eight homebaked pies
And smiled their wobbly sea-leg smiles and tweaked their English
Pleases and thankyous so just a calorie's worth of rich
Accent unidentifiably moneyed and exotic leaked out.
And how but with greed could the rest of us respond
Who stood by the pots and shouted for more boiled meat
And buttersauce as the cruise crowd strolled back
To their grand ship whose pontoons were rumored
Loaded with wonderdrugs none of us could afford nothing
Humans could consume but greed and profit and marketshare
While congress and president wrung their hands and signed
The new national healthcare act for the poor and the elderly
That would be a bitter pill to swallow because the premiums
Would slim a lobsterroll down to its white bun, the co-pay
Would thin a seafood chowder down to soup crackers, deductibles
Would cost a hookarm and a pegleg and a fishing boat and they
Were sorry it was the best they could do because they couldn't
Contain the cost of drugs no they couldn't contain the cost
Of those drug-running cruiseships with bank accounts offshore
No they couldn't throw a half-hitch around that thing
Tow it into port flush out those fat tourists on board
Lobsterbib them stick little red forks in their stubby fingers
Surround them with nutcrackers butterdishes lemon wedges
Little condiments and then in enormous pots boil them.

MEADOW COVE COTTAGE, DEER ISLE, MAINE

Last year I came alone to finish a last draft
of a book with no deadline, the beginning
of late middle age, the osprey cry
overhead for my ears only.

This year I can compose nothing –
my daughter singing Madonna in the shower,
my wife scheduling the days in paradise,
ordering lobsters at the pound, a whale-watch,
a bird-walk, her lovely voice on the phone.

My mantic writing table wobbles
on its wicker legs. My daughter says,
let's gather blueberries. My wife says, let's discover
clams bubbling in the mudflats. Summer comes

unglued from routine, the Maine
pines shine. Laughing gulls cry outside.

Last year, I watched for hours the osprey's
gyroscopic motions, how it kept
its center, its surveying eye,
no matter how the gusts undercut it –

then, the flash of talons, the abrupt
drop, the fish whose fate had come to an end,
the flat rock where it flew to devour its meal.

At another spot, an eagle
seemed tethered to its aerie, all day
plunging the surf for fish, flapping back
to the nest where fledglings

angled their dark mouths. Binoculars let me watch
her tear meat with a yellow beak and
a measured, bloody eye.

I've read that eagles mate in mid-air,
copulate as they fall, and in the mad rush
of such feathery clasp and company, sometimes
seem to forget their solitary natures,

orgasm, swoon, and crash into the sea.

ICED TEA, DEER ISLE, ONE YEAR LATER

1.

All week I came looking for you, Will and Sarah.
Your assistant made my iced tea, a slapdash affair.
She was reading Tom Robbins, a later, sorrier book I didn't
recognize.
The blurbs kept going back to *Even Cowgirls Get the Blues*,
as if the latest novel were faking it, using the bright formulations
of the first, sassy West Coast book, spoken in second
person to the irrepressible hitchhiker, you, Sissy Hankshaw,
now reduced to an aging formula. I was sad to see it.
Sadder not to find you, Will, or you, Sarah,
at the café, where I'd found you every morning last summer,
depending on your talk to breach the silence
surrounding my work. Last summer I had come alone
to finish a book, looking out the harbor window
at osprey and eagle to measure the strength of a line.
They each had a severe eye, the eagle's yellow and critical,
the osprey's white with scorn.
You, Will, made the day easier with your recitations of Rilke,
your salt talk
of his solitude at Duino, overlooking the Adriatic, scratching
lines
equal to the tide's pull, the dazzling aquamarine, the horizon's
separation.
Your friends in Arizona, Dubie and Rios, had given you books
to sell
at the shop. Somehow, they weren't right for this sea-fogged isle,
you said,
and besides, there was Rilke to contend with, the only poet
on your shelf.
The rest was dazzling jewelry you and Sarah made from
precious metals and stones.
Sarah, you talked less, often merely gazed at me and

nodded what you understood.
You had a West Coast mystery, a mind that loved the
unaffected wisdoms of Kabir,
the cold distances in Li Po, the terrifying solitude in Rilke.
But you loved best the comic
sadness of Ghalib, how he served the you of every perfumed
beauty who beckoned
and spurned him, and served the You who never acknowledged
his presence
yet for Whom he bowed and sang. You loved exacting detail,
the exact blend,
for instance, of hibiscus flower, black leaf, and cinnamon
I loved for my iced tea.
Every day last summer you made it… in between polishing
a bracelet, setting a gem.
You asked about my wife and child in Vermont. *If you weren't*
taken… you joked,
if you weren't already taken… You and Will talked of the
dangers
of long distance love, how sometimes you were as separate
as desert dryness
and coastal fog. Above all, stand guard over each other's
solitude, you both said,
pointing to Rilke's elegies, set between bracelets of Navajo
turquoise and green sea glass.

2.

On the first day the cafe is closed, the next open, your
special blend,
hibiscus and black tea, more bitter and black than I remember.
So it goes, all week, your young assistant serving me tea,
my wife coffee, my daughter lemonade.
At week's end, I stop in a last time.
You're there, Sarah, busy with customers.
I'm not sure you remember me. When you look up,
your smile says *yes*. And sadness: the distance

was too great, you say, between the desert and the seacoast.
I still have Rilke on the shelf. Will would have wanted it.
        And you?
I've been in town all week, I say. I'm leaving today.
You wince. Today? Why didn't you come see me?
I did, I did. But I saw only your assistant… the one reading
        Tom Robbins.
But I've been here all week, you say, and wince again,
and smile: Tom Robbins has turned into a terrible novelist…
Why didn't you come? This is bizarre. I know it, you know it.
That wince. Is what. Exactly? Exactly. That wince is
what it is. And my stomach crumbles, my heart hurts,
I'm hopeless and compromised and struck. I had not known
I would go to any level of abstraction not to say
what is staring me in the face, invisible, and enormous.
I will do anything not to say the unsayable. Anything.
Let me introduce you to my wife, I say, and watch her
wince once more before her face sets like a piece of sea
glass clamped into the empty space of a ring.

ONE LAST THING

I forgot to tell you how the seacoast came apart.
Was it the pink sweater, the red lobster claw, the rose sunset
that quickened my pulse and made me make a mess of shellfish?

On the cottage deck overlooking the rising tide
I brushed away mosquitoes to kiss your neck and rub my nose
in blond hair going gray and gradually move my fingers down

to that salty spot where the moans begin. The lightning bugs
were crazy in their yellow-green coming-out among the rosa
        rugosa.
The bay swelled, the lobsters sang, the loons dove, a lone

foghorn warned of ships coming apart on the reefs.
We stumbled toward the bed, long married, laughing at
        the oysters
or briny air responsible for our happy irresponsibility.
        One last thing

that might have asked for a measured reply – a phone call,
        an email
response before dawn – was cancelled by a laughing gull,
        case closed
in a clam shell, memo unwritten on a lobster claw,
        bedsheet-mizzens and bedpost masts

and the storm-tossed calls: all hands on deck.

THE PREPARATION

What a great white
heron
will do for the man
preparing
for surgery, for the chemist's
haymaker, the happy
pink clouds
on the ceiling, the ultra happy
scrubbery of OR,
the matching gleam
of gurney, surgical
tools, surgeon's eye.

There's this long floating at the center
of disbelief
a quarter turn
away from sliced muscles
and nerves,
saw, drill and hammer
cracking
femur and socket,
tapping into place
titanium and plastic
oh my body
what art thou?
where art thou
while Audubon's exact strokes
on a heron's wings
float at the center of attention,
calling from a high wall
confidence, condolence
at once
in the outcome
out the income, coming in

over open ocean, floating

over clouds, white
feathers fragile with
angel light

set against low coastal towns under stormclouds
where nothing perfect has ever
risen from human

action, but
the great white heron's
gleaming eye, white
wings, now there
is accomplishment
like the selfless movement
of the scalpel
through white flesh
drill bit in bone
saw through femoral head
floating, disengaged
for the first time
from my human skeleton,

floating free of socket and joint
that has marked the site
of pain

all these years,
a lance, barb, spear beak, just so
that lifted me from myself
and showed me myself

stuck on a spit
and now, free of it,
floating out, way
out to the white breakers

where the surgeons gather,
scalpels poised, muscles
drawn back, bones ex-
posed, too late now to choose

anything but this
appointed hour
when Audubon's great
white heron turns
back to its calling
disappears into
the frame of the salt
marsh and spears
its first flesh of the day

FROM HAYDEN'S SHACK, I CAN SEE TO THE END OF VERMONT

I shall have given willingly my eyes
their long holiday.
JOHN MILTON

Hunkered here, mid winter,
Clay Hill hollow,
Johnson, Vermont, along
a cold stretch of roiling
water, it gets dark early.
The darker it gets,
the farther I see.
Mind's eye adjusts
its aperture, just as
this old dairy state's
adjusting – just fine,
thanks! – packing up
its milk and maple buckets,
parceling farms, plunking down
silver in the shape
of ski chalets, new bridges
and ridgeroads to get there.

They're moving higher up.
Ayup. This state's adjusting
fine to darker doings,
coating itself in silver.
Make no mistake,
it's getting darker.
No real surprise God's
proverb – *And lo! Your hoards*
of silver shall turn to tears –
comes flooding home.
Mid winter, this much rain
makes silver of Vermont.

Maples buckle under
ice coats. Regal
and ruined. Not
a bucket of sap
come spring.

Highwater mark's set
for erasure. Mind
shapes matter,
and the matter here's
a new (bank)roll of images
washing over the old, images
developed in the mind's
darkest rooms, under-
exposed, over-developed.
Hung on a nail, the picture
shows landscape awash in cash.
Don't stand on my word.
Stand behind the lens and look
for yourself. Is that a silver
maple or silver
girder rising
across the river?

One county over,
in the exploding
suburbs, one mayor
is Marxist, another Progressive.
Here, for now, we vote
Cowshit Farmer. Happiest
when old Hippies and Yankees
shovel shit together,
know cowshit from bullshit
imported from elsewhere.
But even here, it's
darkening. Rising
real estate. High
balls at five.
We close our eyes

to the tale of two cities
nearby, Queen and Capital.

"People's Republic
of Burlington," old Marxist
stronghold, now just a stage
on its way to high
capitalism. Church
Street commodified.
Out on the loop roads
of Montpelier, what does "strip
development" strip? Grass
from pastures, cows
from barns, moss
from stone. Strips
the locals of control,
strips "the local" from our minds:
local color washed, rinsed, blanched.
In the mind's eye, silver
replaces it: silver girders

rising across a lake in Milton
(namesake of paradise lost). An empire –
plastics, this time – pledges its suspension
bridge across clear water.
The tax base wobbles and swallows
its last helping of hemlock. It's getting dark.
Vermont sports thirty new girders, silver
"reinforced structures" replacing
the wooden ones. Is that the silver
side of a brook trout
nailed to a wooden plaque?
Is that the silver
sky of an ice storm moving in?
Ice storms are so New Jersey,
so Connecticut. It's getting dark.
Down here in this hollow,
we're already saying grace.

for Hayden Carruth

A LITTLE CORNY

I'm back in Hayden's writing shack, irascible
and uncharitable as Hayden when work's waylaid
by unplanned visitations. I'm chatting
with Wes McNair and Sebastian Matthews, trading
stories, instead of writing poems, about Carruth,
his several lines of work in Johnson, Vermont –
gardening and haying, repairing Marshall
Washer's tractor or bailer, milking cows and mucking
out stalls, banging out a writer's hack work,
nickel-per-word, review after review, after which, finally,
came the snow-sober or spring-drunk poems.
Then we walk the quarter-mile
to Hayden's old meadow, a lovely
little piece of land by an oxbow on Foote Brook,
where Hayden used to garden and tend
his apple trees. Several thick-barked old ones
are blooming now, alive with bees.
Wes and Sebastian lean in and part
the blossom from the sting, gather bouquets
from the brook-side trees, from what might have been
Hayden-inspired blossoms – honorifics
to a man who would have said, hell and
cunctation, that's as corny as roses in a patch of marigolds
to keep the bugs from busting up the vegetables!

EXCORIATING GHOSTS

June's consuming,
stripping down darkness
to its thinnest hours,
swallowing sleep. Not
the fireflies, not the moon,
not the deer stripping
apple trees, not the cemetery
stones beyond them, are as ravenous
for my wakefulness.

First light and the Harvard landscaper
comes to plan dawn memories
for this place – "a past
you'd have planted had you lived
here last century." So,
apple rows, lone maple
in the field, low stonewalls
along the meadow's fringe…
and were it possible, the whole
site tinted in daguerreotype…

By noon, the brass
knocker, brilliant sunlight, and Waldo,
the town's oldest drunk and
bricklayer, whose chimneys are guaranteed,
he says, to outlast him. A hundred years
ago, says Waldo, your land was town
center, those crossroads outside your door
the hub, Ben Ober and Cemetery roads.
Ben Ober, the most feared logger
in the county, but his industry
kept the townsmen alive until they died,
and went down the other road to the plot
cemetery, just there beyond your apples.

Ayup, too many bugs down by the river,
so folks moved higher up where the breezes
kept them only half crazy from black flies.
And right there on the corner stood a general
store, a tall farmhouse nextdoor, two barns,
three outbuildings. And that farmhouse stood
until the second world war called those farmboys away
and returned them so lazy we bore them
straight to the cemetery over there,
the honored dead of Johnson, Vermont.

By ten o'clock twilight, Waldo
fits the last brick, picks up
his pay, snorts at the Ivy Leaguer's
plans, and scrams, shouting back,
"The winds are so big here
the last house lasted only thirty
years. But my chimney's
still standing. Anyway,
thanks for the drinkin money!"

So, this land's been spoken for.
And Waldo's words are stronger
than any surviving chimney –
the kind that usually says
a home, tumbled or burned, once stood here –
his words opened the past, welcomed
the ghosts, and made it too late
for dreaming "mown corridors" through highgrass
and "pasture rooms" where a picnicking family
with a thatched basket of bleu cheese and Chablis
might spread its blanket and make its ample table.

No, June says join the night
thinning between one day and another,
join the stories older than yours,

in which the nightdeer coring the apples
and stripping the trees come forward as
excoriating ghosts whose harsh breaths
say *Shame!* or *Live!* when the wind comes up,
and blow what's left of the plot cemetery's
breath into these fields – and the deer go on
grinding their jaws, and the full moon
goes on behind clouds, and the night sky
is both overcast and bright enough
to see ghosts by but not bright enough to see
beyond them toward the land's future shape.

THE PERCH

I, too, hate the *stately* in my double-row of pines
that line the county road and slope down
from the icy crest of Clay Hill,
to the iced falls of Foote Brook.

And I detest the *bend* of birch and poplar,
bowing under stiff winds from the cliffs of Laraway,
enormous white hems of snow sweeping regally
around north pasture. And those mossy escutcheon

embroidered on every boundary stone or ancient crab apple,
marking the divisions of an estate – I can almost see
the question mark in a red squirrel's tail or its black eye
regarding me, its mouth full of cold apple. Or the mocking
curtsy in a blue jay's bob as it plunders the winter fruit.

Yes, I hate the *stately*, the *bowing* and *scraping*,
but I do own this affection for higher places, perches
toward which the crows return at day's end, winter flocks
        straggling
back in ragged threes and fives, until a hundred strong

they gather in the pines beyond my home for warmth,
        as northern
lights shimmer stained-glass colors against a high black vault,
and later in the earth's rotation, the spinning signet hand
of eastern light wakes the crows and sends them sailing
off in black armadas toward the day's ordinary treasures...

THE PERFUMED BURN

Fall morning after rain, corner of the porch, a web
of desiccated flies, the spider, her back burdened with eggs.
Between flag-stones, sandy anthills, ants hauling aphids
down into the underworld to suck them dry. Thunder
rumbles on the mountain, moving off, the last lightning
bolts of summer gone. In the garden, cabbage leaves riddled
with moths, mites on tomatoes. Everything with a mouth
        must eat,
must drink the life from the smallest Christ. I rake the detritus
of the day, fallen sunflowers, paper-thin vines of beans, husks
of corn, drooping stalks of fennel, and begin the perfumed burn.
Once in the intricate web of gods, Prometheus was caught,
his liver plucked for his forethought, his fire-theft. I watch
        the flames
wither what's left of withering, watch the next flames-to-be, fall
leaves, flame in the trees. Demeter frets. Persephone waves
and turns away. The maples convert their sugar, flame and flame.

CLUSTER FLIES

clustering in the cool of autumn
all day brazenly sunning
on the gray clapboards of my home
they squeeze in toward sundown
under screen through window seam
so tight black magic couldn't crack it
my white walls blacken with them
my lights burn with their buzzing
the unevolved eye in my brain
tracks them like omens
the house will grow smaller
the sunporch dark with their slaughter
to be vacuumed with the dust
swept up like leaves
or laughed at – their stupid back
spins in an oblong of sunlight
dozing in a cold half world
at the mercy of every creature
who will deny them spring

LATE SEPTEMBER

Last night's puddles instarred
with icy bubbles and faults...
as if heat's still trapped there
between the frozen spaces.
Today, clouds hurry across the sky
toward their erasure. Sunlight strobes
up-meadow, winks at my window, and
flashes to the next hillside. An Arctic gust
lifts my shades and riffles my writing paper.
Now's the season when apples bobble and fall
in the orchard and wind plucks the weakened leaves.
Now's the season when fisher cats cross
the lawns and take a few house cats along.
This is the season Li Po lamented when leaves
scud over ice like lost boats. Listen:
their hulls still scratch the ice with a
tremulous message: the great migrations
are underway: hawks and monarchs,
songbirds and dragonflies join
your loved ones going away, a
daughter's flight to college, a wife's
to fieldwork in the South Seas
where her "human subjects" have never
seen ice. So this is the cold
we call the "empty nest." Blacken
the eye of anyone who says it lightly.
What's left is feather-fluff, soft
and painful to the touch. Flown south,
she steers her fieldwork into its 20th year;
the islanders still smile when she arrives.
Across seasons and distances, she tells me,
they imagine her as something changeless,
suspended, until she returns. Today,
her warmth ascends south of the equator,

while here, she's a sunny memory
stored under the ice that seems
to close over me this morning:
My daughter, too, skates over.
I hear the leaves above me
scratching their messages in passing.

BLUSTERY

Blustery 25-below, O Walt, I wouldn't go
And live with animals tonight –
Or anytime soon. How do
They survive in their snowy lairs?
How could I, for that matter, who
Hasn't taken the wild Swedish plunge
Every chilly night to thicken my fur layer
By layer, I who doze by the fire
With the phone to my ear,
Doze the whole new year
Listening to my wife in such weird
Zone-warping tropical heat, naked,
Whispering her desire for 50-below,
If it brings her home. That's fur
Of a different nature, Walt, layer
Upon layer of love that glows, grows
Over us like a sun-lit coat.
O we are hothouse flowers, Walt,
Naked and limply alive in a narrow
Equatorial zone. Otherwise, we die.
Walt, we must make do
With our lovely human hair.

FIX THE DAMN DOOR!

That goddamn hinge has squealed
Like an unlubricated pig
Since summer. All it takes is –
I have neither the language nor the skill
To tell you what it takes!
Those hinges, flanges, double-hung things –
Those brass concatenations
Holding the bolts – or whatever
The metal locked in those squeaky clasps –
Spray it with WD40! Spray away
Every goddamn problem! I must learn
To fix it, that damn thing
Squealing all night because
I cannot stop it – so
It squeals and squeals as if
In my head, unwilling to be
Reasoned with, just piercing me
All night, as I stumble from
Desk to bed and bed to desk –
That door squealing in or out
Of my imaginings – I imagine
Gary Snyder fixing his leaky roof
By moving a single board – what a Zen
Guy. Can I be that mindful, master
The squeaky, broken piece
Of machinery? Fix the damn
Door, the complaint, heart-
Wrenching, each time I stagger in
And out, all night, at a loss
For words, hankering.

SUGAR MAPLE, AMERICAN BEECH, POISON NIGHTSHADE, AS ANDY GOLDSWORTHY PROJECTION

Was it really there, the installation in the woods?
Yes, the bolus of limbs and vines twined into a woody
ball had intention written all over it. But would he,
like a swinger of birches, bend the nearby beech
into faux arches going back and back into the forest,
until the eye was tricked into seeing every bent stick
as semiotic? Limbs fallen sideways against their trunks,
were they natural or marshalled? I could not say. And would he
have stacked twigs in the hollows of sugar maples
along the trail, or was that the trajectory of a tree,
the natural path of its downward spiral? I could see
nothing clearly, not the forest for the trees,
nor its inverse. It was the curse of a Goldsworthy
caper, as subversive to the system as the nightshade
I came upon, finally, in a pasture beyond the woods –
housed in a small gambrel structure, like a latticed
barn, no screw or nail, just piled together, as if planed lumber
had fallen from a tree. Through the trellis, I could see
the poison nightshade uncoiling its tendrils,
squeezing its berries through the lattices
into the oldest disguise – *come eat of the fruit* –
toward what design I could, for once, foresee.

DAY STAR

(after T'ao Ch'ien)

By noon, my back hurts
in a good way. Shovel soil,
heave rock, rake manure.
Clarify the daystar with a hoe.
Black flies, deer flies.
So the day goes, my shadow
moving beside me. Squash
mounds, carrot rows.
Pie-tins bang their stakes. Birds scatter.
Wind: sun: cloud: sun: wind.
Late day, the moon is
a sickle, a ladle, a smile.
Later, my back hurts worse.
Soon enough, I'll be done
with hurting. For now,
let the day star brighten
each object – rock, squash, man –
and keep it from its shadow

STONE IN A STREAM

Stone in a stream. Man on a stone.

How can words contain them? A green sound
in the brain – *dappled shade* – covers them.
Small holes in poplar leaves cause all that talk and stir.
So long to say it.

Brook trout invisible in sun. But their bones cast shadow
on quartz veins. There's a certain way an eddy
curls and undercuts a current.

I'm leaning back on an old boulder in the stream,
old enough for moss and lichen to make
their little piles of soil. Some slim
green thing lifts out of it, a single stalk
with arrow-leaves, lifting upward.

I crush it when I lean back to view the sky. All that time.

What was its name? Is there no message
but how the shush and thrum of a stream
act on a sympathetic system to stun it into silence?

Beside my left ear, the brook sounds like something that does not
ripple or tumble. Too late for words, a white noise
with whitewater in it scumbles pine-smell, washes over
the ovenbird's song, erasing and erasing. My mind is a green fern,

shadow-bone of an invisible trout on a bottom stone.
A granite flume. A slick pool of quartz light.

I look at the empty space where water curves under a bank.
I look at a black weasel emerge under a towering fern.
I look again at the fern, the banked curve, the empty space.

It never had a name.

BLACKFLY POETICS

The way a blackfly egg spawned
on rock near fast-moving water
becomes the larva spiraling out, rolling over the edge
from its airy world into roiling cold,
takes an air-bubble down, down,
where it becomes its next
best self clinging like a piece of green
moss to a watery bottom-stone, cold time
washing its globed home, until time bursts
the pupal sac, and it rides that dome of air
to surface and dries its wings –

well, that's how I go about it, thought spawned
by whatever comes into focus, leaf or stone,
frozen for a moment from the swirl
of what goes by, then I roll over the edge
into the swirl, the undesirable cold
outside of time and space, the underside
of matter where it starts to effervesce –
when I've had enough, can stand the cold
loneliness no longer, release
on that very bubble of discovery
on which I went down and surface

to bring back the bite and sting that bothers us all.

Photo courtesy of The INN and Celebration of Expressive Arts, Montgomery Center, Vermont

NEIL SHEPARD has published five books of poetry: *Scavenging the Country for a Heartbeat* (First Book Award, Mid-List Press, 1993); *I'm Here Because I Lost My Way* (Mid-List, 1998); *This Far from the Source* (Mid-List, 2006); *(T)ravel / Un(t)ravel* (Mid-List, 2011) and a chapbook, *Vermont Exit Ramps* (Big Table, 2012). His poems appear in literary magazines such as *Boulevard, Harvard Review, New England Review, North American Review, Ploughshares, Paris Review, Shenandoah, Southern Review*, and *Triquarterly*, as well as online at *Poetry Daily, Verse Daily*, and *Poem-a-Day* (Academy of American Poets). He directed the BFA Writing Program at Johnson State College for many years before his retirement in 2009. He also founded the Writers Program at the Vermont Studio Center and directed it for eight years. He currently teaches in the low-residency MFA Writing Program at Wilkes University (PA), and he is the founder and long-time editor of *Green Mountains Review*.